We Are Still Here!

We Are Still Here!

Native American Truths Everyone Should Know

TRACI SORELL

Illustrated by FRANÉ LESSAC

INDIGENOUS
PEOPLES'
DAY
PRESENTATIONS
TONIGHT

ini Charlesbridge

Our Native Nations have always been here. We are Indigenous to the continent now called North America. Our leaders are sovereign and have power to make rules. Our ways of life changed when white people arrived from Europe.

In 1776, white people broke free from England and created their own country called the United States of America, which affected our lives even more. Like European rulers before them, the leaders of the new US government signed legal agreements called treaties with our Native Nations. These treaties recognized the sovereignty of our Native Nations to exercise control and power over our people and lands.

But some treaties forced Native people to leave our homes or sell the lands where our ancestors lived. The US government made promises to Native Nations in almost four hundred treaties altogether. But the federal government did not always keep its promises to the tribes. Most of the time, their laws and policies have been devastating.

Most people do not know what happened to Native Nations and our citizens after treaty making stopped in 1871.

Despite the continued occupation of our homelands,
regular attacks on our sovereignty,
and being mostly forgotten in US culture,
Native Nations all say,

"We are still here!"

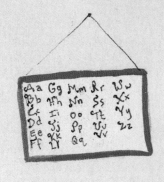

Even under these harsh laws, Native Nations say,

"We are still here!"

ALLOTMENT

White people wanted to control and sell even more of our tribal lands. Native Nations had already given up larger pieces of land for smaller ones in treaties.

In fact, the United States passed laws that

. . . divided up the remaining allotted lands of many tribes.

. . . gave a certain amount of land to each tribal citizen.

. . . sold the "leftover" land to white settlers and railroad companies.

In spite of all this, Native Nations say,

"We are still here!"

Tazbah's Presentation

INDIAN NEW DEAL

The US government tried to help many people during the Great Depression, but its leaders saw how badly Native people suffered compared to others.

Knowing that, Congress crafted a series of new laws that

. . . protected tribal culture, arts, and crafts.

. . . allowed Native languages and traditions to be taught in schools.

. . . set aside money to buy back lost tribal lands.

. . . changed most tribes' governing systems to operate more like the US government, which was not always helpful.

Noting these new laws, Native Nations say,

"We are still here!"

TERMINATION

In order to save money, the US government decided to stop honoring treaty agreements with more than one hundred Native Nations. This terminated our relationship with the federal government and no longer allowed our tribes or citizens to be legally separate in the United States.

Although our tribes kept their part of each treaty, the United States

. . . stopped working with the tribal leaders.

. . . sold the affected Native Nations' lands and resources.

. . . lowered the government's financial duty to tribes nationwide.

With the return of these anti-sovereignty policies, our Native Nations say, **"We are still here!"**

RELOCATION

The federal government wanted us to leave our tribal lands and live and act more like white people.

So Congress passed a law that

. . . pushed aside the fact that Indigenous people are separate under the law, with rights as citizens of our Native Nations and of the United States.

. . . encouraged us to move to cities far from our tribal homes.

. . . promised jobs and schooling to those who moved.

. . . led to populations of poor Native people with little support in cities and suburbs.

14

Even with our people scattered throughout the country,
Native Nations say, **"We are still here!"**

15

TRIBAL ACTIVISM

Native citizens continued to speak up, organize, and increase our long-standing commitment to

. . . strengthen tribal sovereignty.

. . . speak out about termination and relocation.

. . . recover our lands and harvest traditional foods.

. . . draw attention to Native peoples' lack of sufficient health care.

. . . help students go to college, including on tribal lands.

With our collective voice and presence, Native Nations say,
"We are still here!"

SELF-DETERMINATION

Native Nations needed more control of our own lives, so we pushed back on federal rules that oversaw nearly every part of life on our lands.

To support tribal sovereignty, the United States passed laws that

. . . recognized that our governments could handle our own affairs.

. . . helped Native Nations offer programs and services directly to our citizens.

. . . restored many terminated tribes to federally recognized status.

. . . allowed some tribes to recover lands lost during allotment and termination.

While pressuring Congress to carry out
these laws, our Native Nations repeatedly say,
"We are still here!"

INDIAN CHILD WELFARE & EDUCATION

Native Nations care about the welfare and education of our children. We needed to stop officials in various states from removing thousands of our children from their families and placing them in non-Native homes.

Native Nations prompted Congress to approve laws that

... blocked state officials from taking our children without notifying our tribe.

... focused on Native children staying with family or other tribal citizens.

... addressed the specific education needs of Native children in our communities.

To protect and provide for our future generations,

Native Nations say, **"We are still here!"**

RELIGIOUS FREEDOM

Native people challenged federal and local laws and policies that had banned us from freely practicing our traditional religions.

Native Nations sought help from the US Supreme Court, so that

. . . we could practice our beliefs and ceremonies.

. . . tribes could access sacred sites outside our lands.

. . . tribal citizens could keep and use sacred objects.

When the Court did not support us, Native Nations sought support from Congress to say, **"We are still here!"**

ECONOMIC DEVELOPMENT

Tribal leaders noticed our people failing financially while others in the United States succeeded. Some Native Nations opened casinos as a way to make money on our lands where few opportunities existed.

This type of business allows those tribes to

. . . vary how people earn a living and care for themselves.

. . . use profits to develop businesses and employment.

. . . pay for important services like police, fire stations, and health care.

. . . offer scholarships and after-school programs as well as operate tribally run schools.

Even though the federal government regulates tribal casinos, Native Nations say, **"We are still here!"**

SEAFOOD GRILL

MENU

LANGUAGE REVIVAL

Native Nations want to increase the number of tribal language speakers. This is necessary to pass on values, stories, and ceremonies to future generations.

Seeking to preserve our cultures, Native Nations urged Congress to approve laws to

. . . encourage teaching Native languages in schools.

. . . allow our Native speakers to teach in classrooms.

. . . give financial grants to tribes and schools for language programs.

Speaking Indigenous languages strengthens our heritage,
so each Native Nation says (in our own language),

"We are still here!"

Signs in illustration:
- Defend the SACRED
- WATER IS LIFE
- Indigenous Strength
- NATIVE LIVES MATTER
- INDIGENOUS PEOPLES' MARCH
  BE PART OF THE MOVEMENT
  BE PART OF HISTORY
  BE PART OF THE CHANGE
- SAY NO TO RACIST MASCOTS
- RESPECT INDIGENOUS SOVEREIGNTY

Chance's Presentation

SOVEREIGN RESURGENCE

Having survived disease, war, and federal rules meant to destroy us and our way of life, Native Nations continue to exercise our sovereignty.

Together, we take action to

. . . speak up for the land, water, and resources everyone needs to live.

. . . look after our citizens' health, education, and safety.

. . . share information with the United Nations about our treatment in the United States.

. . . work together to shape federal and state policies that affect our citizens.

All the while we say,

"WE ARE STILL HERE!"

INDIGENOUS PEOPLES' DAY

Assimilation
by Wenona

Allotment
by Kee

Indian New Deal
by Tazbah

Self-Determination
by Will

Indian Child Welfare Education
by DJ

Religious Freedom
by Maya

MORE INFORMATION

The twelve topics in this book are specific to Native Nations' experiences. It's important to know that while some of these topics have specific historical time frames, many are ongoing and all of them still affect Native citizens and Native Nations today.

ASSIMILATION (*pages 6 & 7*): policies that the US government adopted to make Native people part of the dominant white culture; Native people were to speak only English and adopt Christianity ◆ *Illustration*: students from various Native Nations attending Carlisle Indian Industrial School, Pennsylvania, in the early 1900s

ALLOTMENT (*pages 8 & 9*): the act of dividing communal tribal lands owned by Native Nations into plots and assigning them to individual Native citizens to own instead ◆ *Illustration*: an early-1900s Mandan family on their allotted land on the Fort Berthold reservation in North Dakota where Mandan, Hidatsa, and Arikara Nations still live today

INDIAN NEW DEAL (*pages 10 & 11*): federal laws that ended allotment, supported Native cultures and languages, and changed tribal governments to match the systems used by the federal government ◆ *Illustration*: Salish & Kootenai leaders of the Flathead Reservation in Montana receiving the first signed Indian Reorganization Act constitution from US Secretary of the Interior Harold Ickes in Washington, DC, in 1935

TERMINATION (*pages 12 & 13*): federal laws that stopped treating more than one hundred Native Nations and their citizens as Native peoples and also took away their homelands ◆ *Illustration*: citizens of Menominee Tribe in the early 1960s at Legend Lake on their reservation in Wisconsin, protesting the taking of their land as white people fish

RELOCATION (*pages 14 & 15*): a federal program with a goal to assimilate Native people into the larger US population; it moved Native people away from their tribes to cities for low-paying jobs ◆ *Illustration*: a Native family arriving in Denver, Colorado, in the late 1950s

TRIBAL ACTIVISM (*pages 16 & 17*): Native Nations and urban Native people advocating for better treatment and demanding that the US government fulfill treaty obligations and respect tribal sovereignty ◆ *Illustration*: Native people occupying Alcatraz Island off the coast of San Francisco, California, in the 1960s

SELF-DETERMINATION (*pages 18 & 19*): the right of a Native Nation to govern itself and take care of its people; current federal laws encourage tribes (instead of the US government) to provide direct services to their citizens ◆ *Illustration*: an educational hike on the Lookout Trail, Mescalero Apache Reservation, New Mexico

INDIAN CHILD WELFARE AND EDUCATION (*pages 20 & 21*): the Indian Child Welfare Act (ICWA) protects Native children from being removed from their family and tribe and provides them educational opportunities in their tribal communities ◆ *Illustration*: families spending time together at Mashpee Wakeby Pond, Mashpee Wampanoag Tribe, Massachusetts

RELIGIOUS FREEDOM (pages 22 & 23): the American Indian Religious Freedom Act (a resolution, rather than a law) stated that Native peoples have the right to practice their spiritual beliefs ◆ *Illustration*: oral arguments for the 1987 Lyng v. Northwest Indian Cemetery Protective Association case before eight justices in the US Supreme Court concerning sites sacred to the Karuk, Tolowa, and Yurok tribes in Six Rivers National Forest, California

ECONOMIC DEVELOPMENT (pages 24 & 25): actions taken by Native Nations to create jobs and business opportunities for their citizens and others and to raise the quality of life in their communities ◆ *Illustration*: a tribally operated casino in the Pacific Northwest

LANGUAGE REVIVAL (pages 26 & 27): commitment to ensure that Native languages continue by speaking and teaching them in schools and communities, particularly to young people; many Native languages have almost disappeared due to US government policies that prohibited people from speaking them ◆ *Illustration*: students studying the Cherokee language and syllabary at a school within the Cherokee Nation, Oklahoma

SOVEREIGN RESURGENCE (pages 28 & 29): Native Nations exercising political and legal power within the United States and internationally ◆ *Illustration*: Native people participating in an Indigenous Peoples' Day celebration

OTHER INFORMATION

Tribal flags (cover): While flying federal and state flags is common across the United States, the practice of flying the flags of Native Nations has not been as typical. Many tribes do not even have a flag. Some put a government seal on a white or colored background to create a flag. Others design specific images and borders. The flags in this book represent the geographic and cultural diversity of Native Nations across the country.

The school in this book: In some cities, children from different Native Nations attend school together, where Indigenous cultures, languages, and histories are included and centered in their learning.

TIME LINE

The history of relations and treaty making between Native Nations and the United States started when European settlers first arrived in what is now North America. This timeline begins when that treaty making was officially ended by the US government. This is when Indigenous people generally disappear from curriculum.

1870 1800s

1871

President Ulysses S. Grant's signature on the **Indian Appropriations Act** ends US treaty making with Native Nations and creates a focus on one unified national government after the Civil War—without consulting tribal leaders. Despite this, the federal government's responsibility to uphold what it promised in all prior legal agreements remains.

1876

Lakota, Cheyenne, and Arapaho warriors defeat the US Seventh Cavalry led by Lieutenant Colonel George Custer at the **Battle of Little Bighorn** (within the Crow reservation, located in what is now southeastern Montana) on June 25.

1879

The first federally funded off-reservation **boarding school** for Native children opens in Carlisle, Pennsylvania. Federal policies direct churches and missionaries to take Native children away from their tribe and family to be educated in boarding schools, to convert them to Christianity, and to prepare them for manual labor. By 1926, more than 80 percent of school-age Native children attend either religious or non-religious boarding schools.

1900s

1880
1890
1910
1920
1930
1940

1887

Congress passes the **General Allotment Act**, which divides communal tribal lands into plots and gives them to individual tribal members. "Excess" or "leftover" lands are sold to white settlers and railroad companies. More than 90 million acres of tribal lands are taken away from Native Nations.

1890

The US Seventh Cavalry murders Lakota families camped along **Wounded Knee Creek** on the Pine Ridge reservation in South Dakota on December 29.

1898

The **Curtis Act** breaks up the tribal governments and communal lands of the Cherokee, Choctaw, Muscogee, Chickasaw, and Seminole Nations in Indian Territory.

1917–1918

More than ten thousand Indigenous people serve in the US Army and more than two thousand serve in the US Navy during **World War I**.

1921

In the **Snyder Act**, Congress defines the federal government's responsibility to provide services and support to Native people living on reservations and attending government-run boarding schools.

1924

To thank Native people who served in World War I, the **Indian Citizenship Act** is signed by President Calvin Coolidge, granting US citizenship to all citizens of Native Nations. But citizenship does not guarantee the right to vote in several states, including South Dakota, Arizona, and New Mexico.

1941–1945

During **World War II**, more than 44,000 of the 350,000 Native people in the United States enlist. Men from sixteen tribes use their tribal languages to relay coded messages on the battlefield. More than 65,000 Native men and women move to cities to work in the wartime defense industry.

1944

The **National Congress of American Indians** is founded. Today it is the oldest and largest advocacy organization for Native Nations in the United States.

1950   1960   1970

1950–1953

Approximately 10,000 Indigenous people serve in the **Korean War**.

1953

President Dwight D. Eisenhower signs a series of statutes that ends the US government's relationship with more than one hundred Native Nations, removing legal recognition of their governmental status and protections of their land and culture. Federal support for programs and services is stopped even though there are treaties and agreements in place. **Termination** forces many tribal citizens to move because their land no longer belongs to the tribe. The National Congress of American Indians fights against termination and helps some tribes avoid it.

1956

The **Indian Relocation Act** encourages tens of thousands of Indigenous people to move to cities with the promise of employment, housing, and educational opportunities. But many people find themselves with low-paying jobs in poor neighborhoods. Urban Native community centers are founded to provide cultural support for those now isolated from family and tribal homelands. These newly relocated people join the many Native veterans already in cities where they found jobs after their service.

1961

The **American Indian Conference**, hosted by the University of Chicago in cooperation with Native people, drafts the "Declaration of Indian Purpose," calling for the end of termination; recognition of treaty rights; and other federal policies and funding focused on health, education, and safety.

1961–1974

Urban Native people form organizations such as the National Indian Youth Council, the American Indian Movement, Women of All Red Nations, and the International Indian Treaty Council to advocate for Native Nations and their citizens. These collective efforts are known as the **"Red Power Movement."** People write articles and lead protests and occupations to publicize demands.

1964–1975

More than 42,000 Native people join the US armed forces during the **Vietnam War**. The Vietnam Veterans Memorial lists 248 who were killed in action.

1968

President Lyndon B. Johnson delivers his **"Forgotten American" speech** to Congress, aimed at extending his Great Society programs—created to combat poverty and racial injustice—to Native peoples.

1970

President Richard Nixon officially abandons the termination policy and supports self-determination for Native Nations. He signs the **Indian Education Act** in 1972. After asking for decades, the Taos Pueblo people convince President Nixon and Congress to return Blue Lake and 48,000 acres of their traditional lands in New Mexico. This provides a model for Congress to return traditional lands to other Native Nations.

1971

President Nixon signs the **Alaska Native Claims Settlement Act**, which establishes more than 200 Alaska Native corporations and villages. Through the law, they receive 44 million acres of land and nearly one billion dollars. The act also does away with any future title claims to 320 million acres of land in Alaska.

1975

Congress passes the **Indian Self-Determination and Education Assistance Act**. This allows tribes to run some of the programs that the US government's Bureau of Indian Affairs used to operate. Carrying out the law goes very slowly, and tribes continue to advocate for expansion.

1977–1979

Congress creates the **American Indian Policy Review Commission**. It reviews federal rules governing Native peoples' affairs, gathers tribal input, and guides policy-making decisions.

1978

Native Nations and advocates inform Congress about the high number of Native children still being taken from their families and placed with non-Native people. Since these children are dual citizens of their Native Nation and the United States, Native leaders request that the federal government stop states from taking children without involving the tribe and the child's family in legal proceedings. In response, Congress enacts the **Indian Child Welfare Act (ICWA)**.

1978

Native Nations push for protection of their traditional religious practices. The **American Indian Religious Freedom Act** is passed, but it's merely a policy statement. Native Nations and their citizens still have no enforceable way to participate in traditional ceremonies, access sacred sites, or possess sacred objects. Later Supreme Court decisions do not uphold the religious freedom rights of Native citizens.

1988

Tribes have always had traditional games of chance, so some tribes decide to offer casino-style gaming. After the Supreme Court recognizes that Native Nations have the right to operate these games, the federal government passes the **Indian Gaming Regulatory Act**, which forces tribes to negotiate with states and share profits. Today many states receive large payments from tribes each year and benefit greatly from tribal gaming.

1990

The **Native American Languages Act** allows Native languages to be taught in schools. This leads to the Esther Martinez Native American Languages Preservation Act in 2006, which provides funding for tribal language-immersion programs.

1990

Building on earlier advocacy, tribes successfully get Congress to enact the **Native American Graves Protection and Repatriation Act (NAGPRA)**, which requires organizations receiving federal monies to return cultural items and human remains to Native Nations.

2001–PRESENT

More than 22,000 Native people serve in the **US armed forces**, including in Iraq and Afghanistan.

2004

The **National Museum of the American Indian** opens as part of the Smithsonian in Washington, DC, on September 21. Native Nations and Indigenous communities contributed to the design, landscaping, and exhibitions.

2007

The United Nations General Assembly adopts the **Declaration on the Rights of Indigenous Peoples**, which establishes minimum standards for the "survival, dignity, and well-being of the indigenous peoples of the world." The United States is one of only four countries to vote against it but later endorses this important international instrument under President Barack Obama in 2010. Indigenous peoples started advocating for this declaration forty years earlier.

GLOSSARY OF TERMS

There are lots of complex words and terms in this book. Be sure to use your dictionary or search online for more information about anything you want to know more about! Below is what some of these terms mean in the context of this book.

boarding schools: schools operated by the federal government or Christian organizations to assimilate Native children into white US culture

casinos: Native Nation–owned businesses for playing games of chance located on tribal lands

culture: beliefs, practices, and values shared by a group of people

federally recognized status: a term recognizing the government-to-government relationship between a Native Nation and the United States

grants: money supplied by a government or charitable organization for training, services, or programs to assist others

Great Depression: a decade of worldwide economic hard times from 1929 through 1939; many people struggled to find work, pay housing and utility bills, and feed their family

Indian: a historic term that refers to an Indigenous person or tribe, created by Christopher Columbus's error when he thought he was on the Indian subcontinent in Southern Asia

Indigenous: native to a place; also refers to citizens of Native Nations when capitalized

legally separate: a legal description of Native Nations because they existed prior to the creation of the United States; they and their citizens (who are also US citizens) are governed by tribal laws in addition to federal laws

Native Nations: Indigenous peoples separated into distinct tribes with their own governments, languages, and cultures, such as the Cherokee Nation, the Navajo Nation, the Minnesota Chippewa Tribe, and hundreds of other tribes within US borders

occupation: the possession or control of a place, sometimes by force

officials: people who are elected to or work for a government

resolution: a statement or motion by lawmakers (not an enforceable law)

sovereignty: authority over people, land, and resources

treaty: a negotiated legal agreement made and signed by two or more sovereign governments

treaty making: the process of negotiating a legal agreement

tribal citizen: an Indigenous person recognized by and enrolled in a Native Nation

United Nations: an international political organization that helps people around the world; it was created in 1945 and has more than one hundred member countries

SOURCES

Because finding accurate sources about Native Nations can be tricky when searching online, it's a good idea to visit Native Nations' websites for information. Also have a look at the National Museum of the American Indian (americanindian.si.edu) and the national news source Indian Country Today (indiancountrytoday.com).

Fixico, Donald L. *Termination and Relocation: Federal Indian Policy, 1945–1960.* Albuquerque: University of New Mexico Press, 1990.

National Library of Medicine. "Native Voices Timeline." www.nlm.nih.gov/nativevoices/timeline/index.html.

Prucha, Francis Paul, ed. *Documents of United States Indian Policy.* Lincoln: University of Nebraska Press, 2000.

Treuer, David. *The Heartbeat of Wounded Knee: Native America from 1890 to the Present.* New York: Riverhead Books, 2019.

US Department of Health & Human Services. "American Indians and Alaska Natives—The Trust Responsibility." Administration for Native Americans. March 19, 2014. www.acf.hhs.gov/ana/resource/american-indians-and-alaska-natives-the-trust-responsibility.

US Department of the Interior. "Frequently Asked Questions." Indian Affairs. www.bia.gov/frequently-asked-questions.

AUTHOR'S NOTE

All the information on these pages is true—this book is nonfiction. The students giving the presentations in the book are not real, but there are Native-operated schools like the one depicted in this book where young people learn these facts. Everything in this book is a fundamental part of the United States' history, as well as its present, and should be known by everyone living in this country.

I'm a dual citizen of the Cherokee Nation and the United States, so I know the effects that these federal laws and policies have had on my tribe.

As the stories, songs, and writings our ancestors tell us, we Cherokee and other citizens of today's Native Nations have always lived on this continent. Our Indigenous ways of life changed forever when people arrived from European countries. The European men (since all their leaders were men then) carved up the land into colonies and later created new countries. Disease, wars, forced migrations, and death by genocide became a regular part of our reality. The white settlers did not allow women to participate in government (no voting or holding elected office). Their values were not shared by Native Nations.

The Europeans' changes altered our governing structures. Laws and policies were put in place to limit the sovereignty of Native Nations. This made it difficult for us to govern our own people and others who came onto our lands. As the United States grew, the federal government focused on two main goals: gaining control over tribal lands and assimilating Native peoples—trying to force us to become like white people.

I hope this book's text, art, and time line make it clear that Native people have always been actively engaged in protecting our sovereignty and culture. Our advocacy has brought both harm and support from the federal government. Historical records document these facts. Yet, regardless of everything Native people have been through, we remain an integral part of the fabric of the United States. For example, most people are surprised to learn about the high rate of service by Native people in the US armed forces despite how Native Nations have been treated.

This book mostly focuses on actions taken by the executive and legislative branches of the US government. Many decisions about Native Nations and our citizens have also been decided in federal courts since the early 1800s. The US government has a "trust responsibility" to Native Nations—a duty to protect and respect our sovereignty—which has been a critical and complicated part of many of these cases.

With more than 570 tribes inside US borders today, the histories of individual Native Nations' experiences with federal laws and policies also deserve to be known. Whether or not you are a citizen of a Native Nation, I encourage you to research whose ancestral lands you live on and how specific tribes have experienced—and still experience—the laws, policies, and movements included in this book.

Despite all that has occurred since Europeans arrived on this continent, Native Nations proclaim "We are still here!" *because we have survived.* We seek opportunities to thrive and work alongside others to protect the land, water, and other resources everyone depends on to exist on this planet.

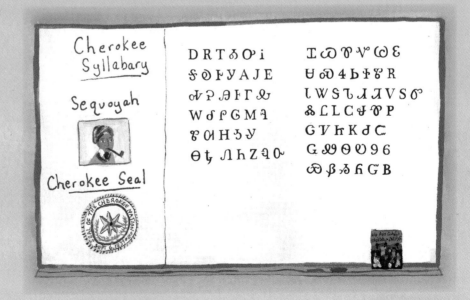

To my teachers: those of family,
community, classroom, and life—T. S.

For Carlos—F. L.

Wado to Professor Kirsten Matoy Carlson of Wayne State University
Law School for her assistance. And no book of mine is ever written
without my family's support, but this one received lots of helpful edits from Carlos—
my all-time favorite editor and beta reader.—T. S.

Thank you to Jim Gerencser, Carlisle Indian School Digital Resource
Center, and Angie Brus and Neal McCaleb, Carlisle Indian School Project,
for their assistance.—F. L.

Published by Charlesbridge · 9 Galen Street, Watertown, MA 02472
(617) 926-0329 · www.charlesbridge.com

Library of Congress Cataloging-in-Publication Data
Names: Sorell, Traci, author. | Lessac, Frané, illustrator.
Title: We are still here!: Native American truths everyone should know / Traci Sorell; illustrated by Frané Lessac.
Description: Watertown, MA: Charlesbridge, [2021] | Includes bibliographical references. | Audience:
Ages 7-10. | Summary: "A group of Native American kids from different tribes
presents twelve historical and contemporary time periods, struggles, and victories to their
classmates, each ending with a powerful refrain: we are still here"—Provided by publisher.
Identifiers: LCCN 2020007134 (print) | LCCN 2020007135 (ebook) | ISBN
9781623541927 (hardcover) | ISBN 9781632899736 (ebook)
Subjects: LCSH: Indians of North America—History—Juvenile literature. | Indians, Treatment of—
United States—Juvenile literature. | Indigenous peoples—United States—Government relations—
Juvenile literature. | Persistence—Juvenile literature.
Classification: LCC E77.4 .S625 2021 (print) | LCC E77.4 (ebook) | DDC973.04/97—dc23
LC record available at https://lccn.loc.gov/2020007134
LC ebook record available at https://lccn.loc.gov/2020007135

Printed in China
(hc) 10 9 8 7 6 5 4 3 2

The illustrations for this book were created with gouache on Arches paper
Display type hand lettered by Ryan O'Rourke, Text type set in Cabrito Norm
Color separations by Colourscan Print Co Pte Ltd, Singapore
Printed by 1010 Printing International Limited in Huizhou, Guangdong, China
Production supervision by Brian G. Walker
Designed by Cathleen Schaad